Oxford Reading Tree

Level 4

Floppy's Phonics

Activity Book

4

Debbie Hepplewhite

OXFORD

| ai | -ay | oi | oy |
| ee | ea | -igh | -ie |

| oa | ow | -ue | ew |
| -oo | -ew | ow | ou |

| ur | ir | or | aw |
| ear | eer | air | -are |

| s | -ce | e | -ea | u |
| o | -ed | -ed | | |

Practise the sounds

a e i o u

s t p n m

Say the sounds. Trace the letters.

set put man pins tops pots

mint stop spin stem mist

snaps spent stump steps

Sound out and blend to read the words.

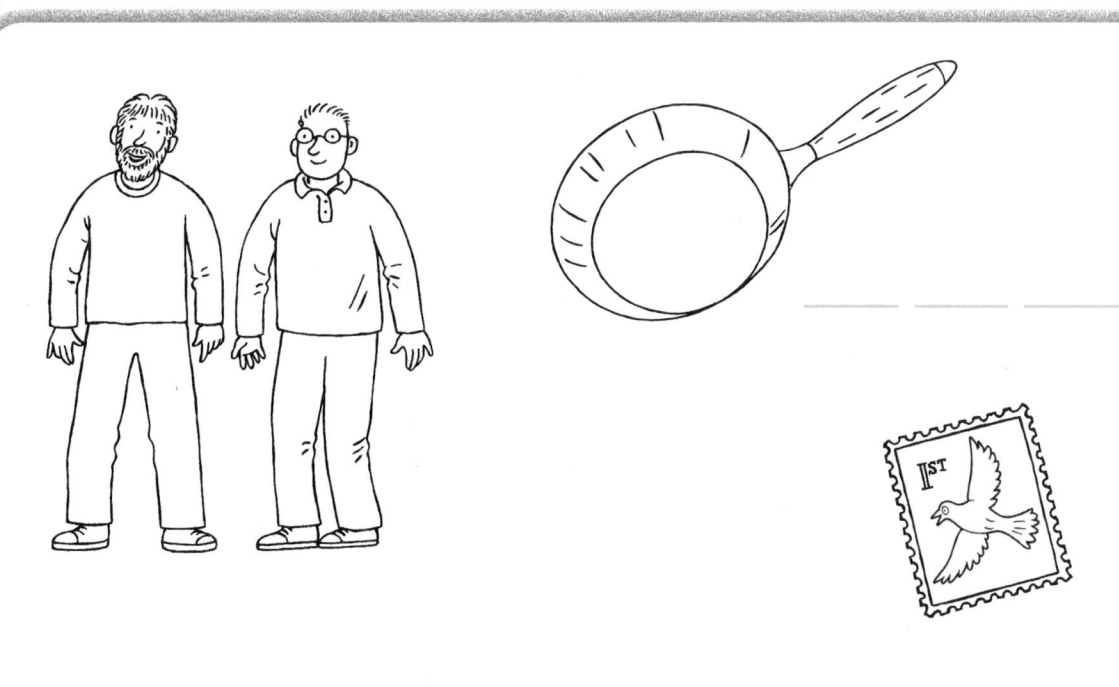

Say the words. Spell the words. Write the words.

2

Practise your reading and writing

Spell and write words with the focus graphemes.

1. Ten men took a tent and set up camp.

2. Biff fell up the step and onto the mat.

Blend to read the words and sentences.

Copy one of the sentences while saying the sounds of the words. Draw a picture to match the sentence.

© Oxford University Press © Phonics International Ltd. 2020

Practise the sounds

d g c k k ck r
a e i o u

Say the sounds. Trace the letters.

dig red duck kid cod rug

kick grid drag rock speck

cracks grand crags strict

Sound out and blend to read the words.

Say the words. Spell the words. Write the words.

Practise your reading and writing

Spell and write words with the focus graphemes.

1. A dog will get in a mess if he digs in the mud.

2. The duck was cross when he got a stick stuck in the mud.

Blend to read the words and sentences.

Copy one of the sentences while saying the sounds of the words. Draw a picture to match the sentence.

Practise the sounds

h   b   f   ff   l   ll   le

ss   a   e   i   o   u

Say the sounds. Trace the letters.
Say the sounds. Trace the letters.

hob   leg   fuss   hill   fell   hiss

bluff   flag   loft   fluff   bells

raffle   lesson   puffin   prickle

Sound out and blend to read the words.

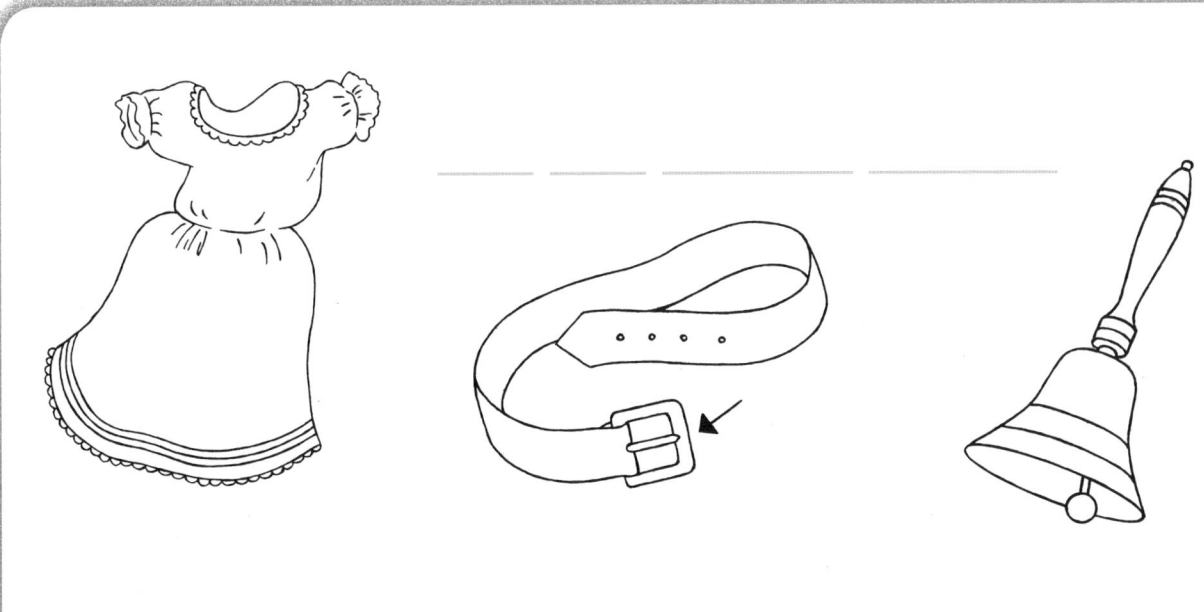

Say the words. Spell the words. Write the words.

Practise your reading and writing

Spell and write words with the focus graphemes.

1. The big hen pecks at her food and then hops off.

2. Biff has a red dress and it has fluff on the hem.

Blend to read the words and sentences.

Copy one of the sentences while saying the sounds of the words. Draw a picture to match the sentence.

Practise the sounds

j v w x y z zz

qu a e i o u

yes yet wig jot vets wax

quiz buzz jazz zips quack tax

yells fizz squid toxic quest

_____

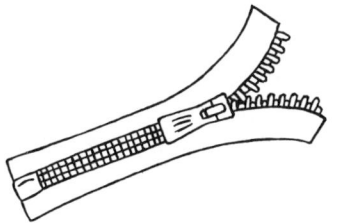

_____   ___ ___ ___

Practise your reading and writing

a e i o u j v
w -x y z -zz qu

Spell and write words with the focus graphemes.

1. Quick, the big bug can buzz and zip and fly up and down.

2. "Pack up all the boxes quickly," said Biff, "we need to go soon!"

Blend to read the words and sentences.

Copy one of the sentences while saying the sounds of the words. Draw a picture to match the sentence.

Practise the sounds

ch sh th
th ng nk

Say the sounds. Trace the letters.

chat shop then crush think

this much push blush thanks

richest length strength chunk

Sound out and blend to read the words.

Say the words. Spell the words. Write the words.

Practise your reading and writing

Spell and write words with the focus graphemes.

1. "I will have fish with my chips not chicken wings, thank you," said Wilma.

2. We go to the park and chat as we swish on the swings.

Blend to read the words and sentences.

Copy one of the sentences while saying the sounds of the words. Draw a picture to match the sentence.

11   © Oxford University Press © Phonics International Ltd. 2020

Practise the sounds

ai ee igh oa

Say the sounds. Trace the letters.

feet   sigh   rain   coat   peel

soaks   tree   lights   paint   stain

speeds   floating   brighten   explain

Sound out and blend to read the words.

_ _ _ _ _ _ _ _

Say the words. Spell the words. Write the words.

Practise your reading and writing

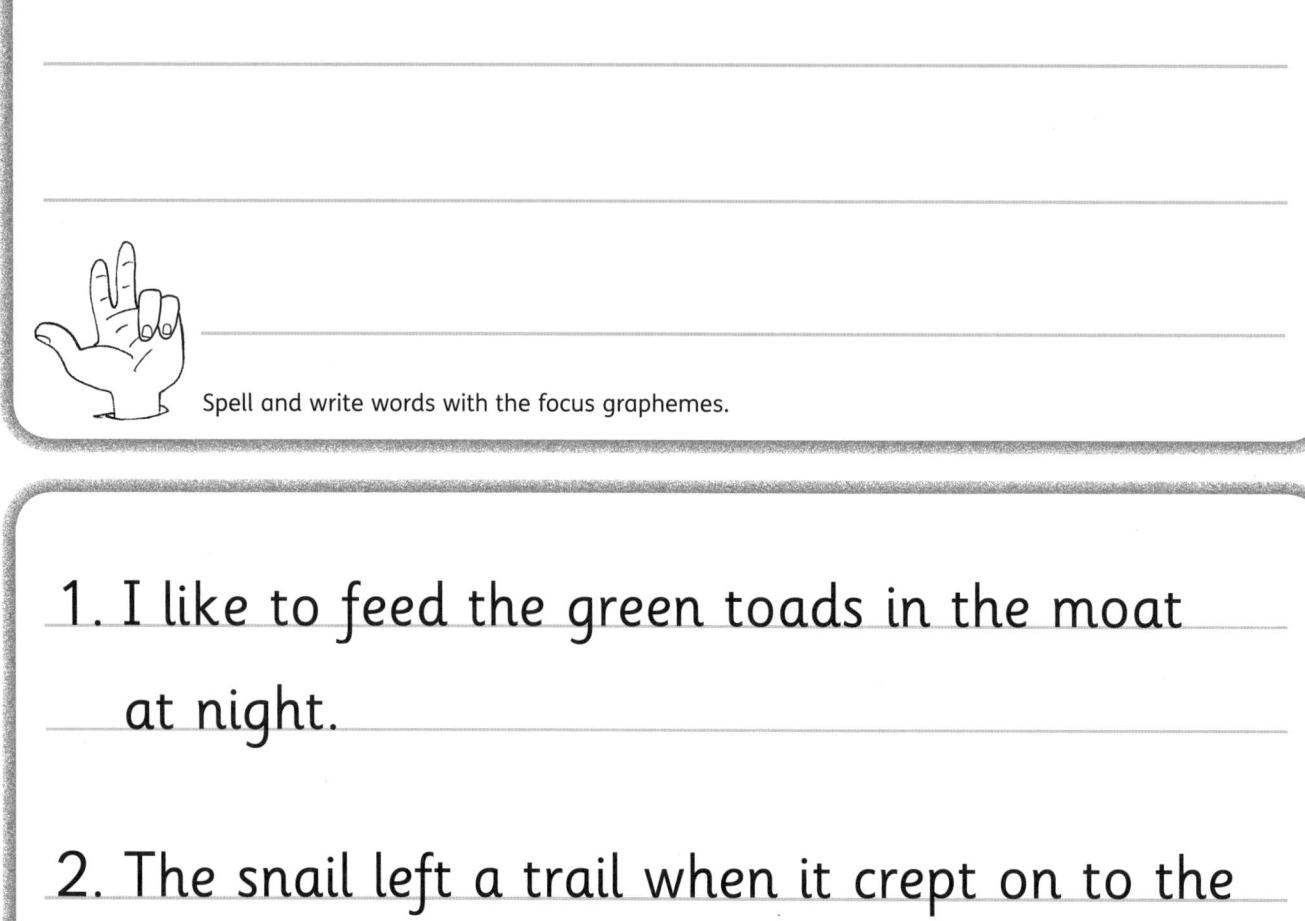

Spell and write words with the focus graphemes.

1. I like to feed the green toads in the moat at night.

2. The snail left a trail when it crept on to the grass in the night.

Blend to read the words and sentences.

Copy one of the sentences while saying the sounds of the words. Draw a picture to match the sentence.

Practise the sounds

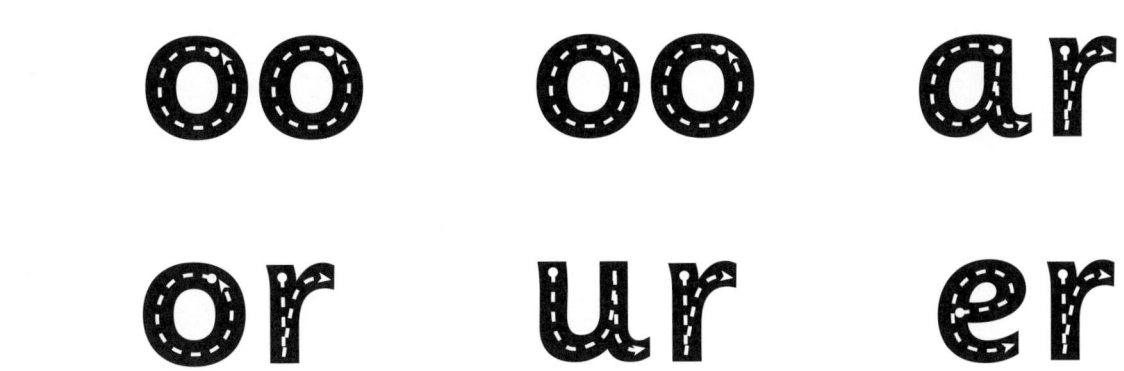

Say the sounds. Trace the letters.

car horn burn moon herd

looks start shorts churn

alarm storm mermaid curls

Sound out and blend to read the words.

Say the words. Spell the words. Write the words.

Practise your reading and writing

Spell and write words with the focus graphemes.

1. Look at the moon – it is not as far as the stars!

2. I took a short trip in a balloon but it burst and we spun to the stars.

Blend to read the words and sentences.

Copy one of the sentences while saying the sounds of the words. Draw a picture to match the sentence.

Practise the sounds

ow   oi   ear
air

Say the sounds. Trace the letters.

now   fear   soil   hair   town

coins   chair   shears   howls

spoilt   beard   avoid   downstairs

Sound out and blend to read the words.

Say the words. Spell the words. Write the words.

Practise your reading and writing

Spell and write words with the focus graphemes.

1. The owl is up high in the air so she cannot join the chick in the clearing.

2. Cows like flowers but they do not like soil.

Blend to read the words and sentences.

Copy one of the sentences while saying the sounds of the words. Draw a picture to match the sentence.

Practise the sound

Say the sound. Trace the letters.

Say the sound. Trace the letters.

pain day wait say snail

may stay away sways tail

playing stray raining Saturday

Sound out and blend to read the words.

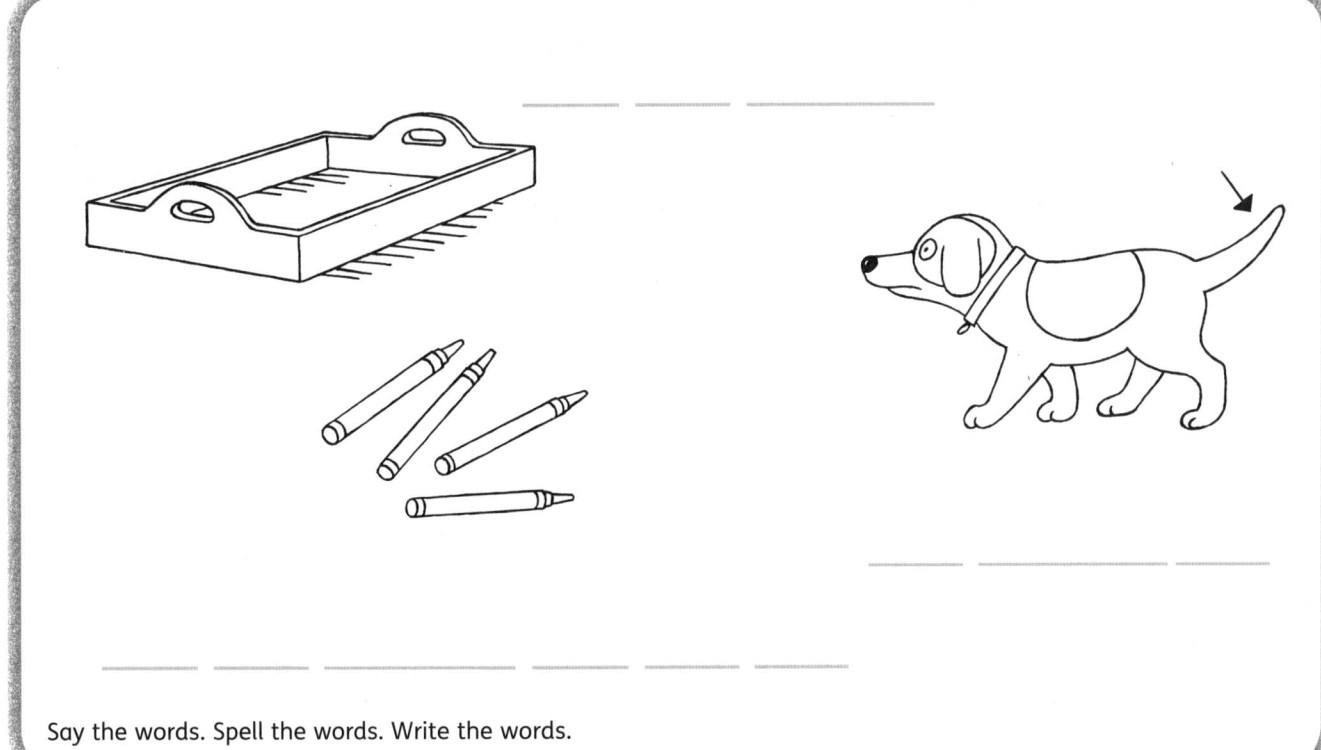

Say the words. Spell the words. Write the words.

Practise your reading and writing

Spell and write words with the focus graphemes.

1. Some trains stay on the platform and some trains zip away.

2. The rain seems set to stay so we must come in to play.

Blend to read the words and sentences.

Copy one of the sentences while saying the sounds of the words. Draw a picture to match the sentence.

Practise the sound

Say the sound. Trace the letters.

Say the sound. Trace the letters.

foil   boy   join   joy   boil   coy

enjoy   toys   annoy   ploy   spoilt

moist   destroy   oysters   ointment

Sound out and blend to read the words.

Say the words. Spell the words. Write the words.

Practise your reading and writing

_____

_____

_____

Spell and write words with the focus graphemes.

1. We join in with the boys' play and bring the
   best toys.

2. The boy was very spoilt and did not enjoy
   playing with children at the park.

Blend to read the words and sentences.

_____

_____

Copy one of the sentences while saying the sounds of the words. Draw a picture to match the sentence.

Practise the sound

Say the sound. Trace the letters.

Say the sound. Trace the letters.

bee   tea   see   sea   tree   eat

team   neat   reach   feast   dream

plea_se_   seal   stream   teacher

Sound out and blend to read the words.

Say the words. Spell the words. Write the words.

Practise your reading and writing

Spell and write words with the focus graphemes.

1. Three of us went to the beach to eat a picnic tea by the sea.

2. We were hidden in a heap of leaves next to a tree and they did not see us!

Blend to read the words and sentences.

Copy one of the sentences while saying the sounds of the words. Draw a picture to match the sentence.

Practise the sound

Say the sound. Trace the letters.

Say the sound. Trace the letters.

tight tie light lie night sigh

flight pie die tied lies fright

dries cries spies untie fries

Sound out and blend to read the words.

_____ _____

_____ _____

Practise your reading and writing

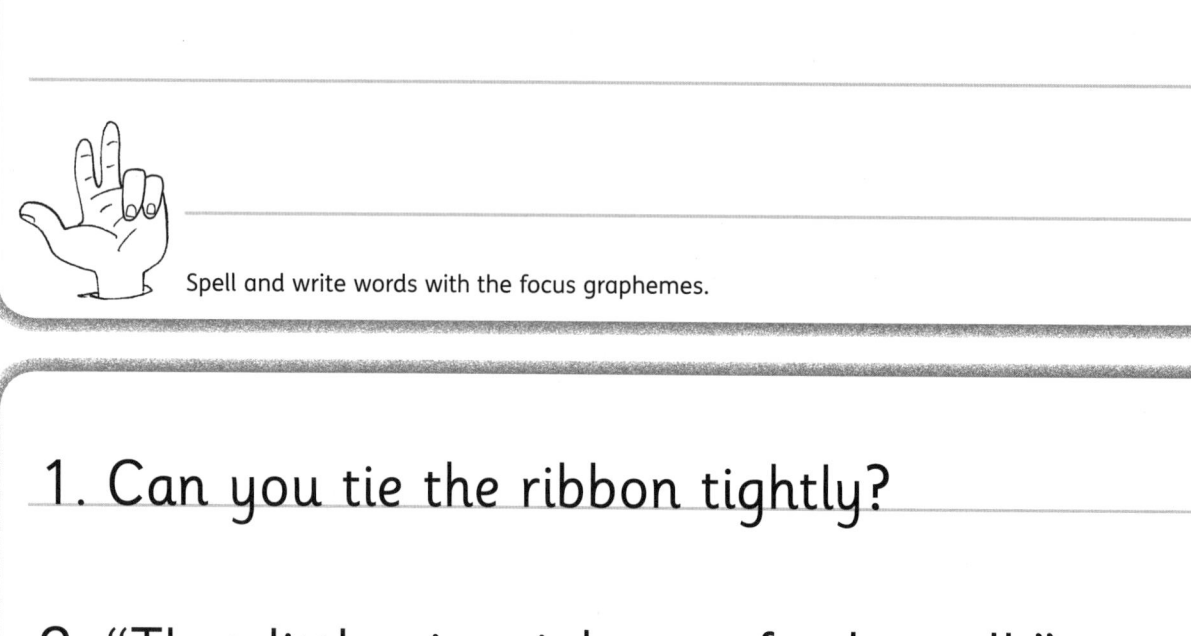

Spell and write words with the focus graphemes.

1. Can you tie the ribbon tightly?

2. "That little pie might not feed us all," said Chip.

Blend to read the words and sentences.

Copy one of the sentences while saying the sounds of the words. Draw a picture to match the sentence.

Practise the sound

Say the sound. Trace the letters.

Say the sound. Trace the letters.

oak   own   soap   row   road   low

float   grow   glows   flown   pillow

snowing   b<u>e</u>low   yellow   blow

Sound out and blend to read the words.

_ _ _ _

_ _ _ _

_ _ _ _ _

Say the words. Spell the words. Write the words.

Practise your reading and writing

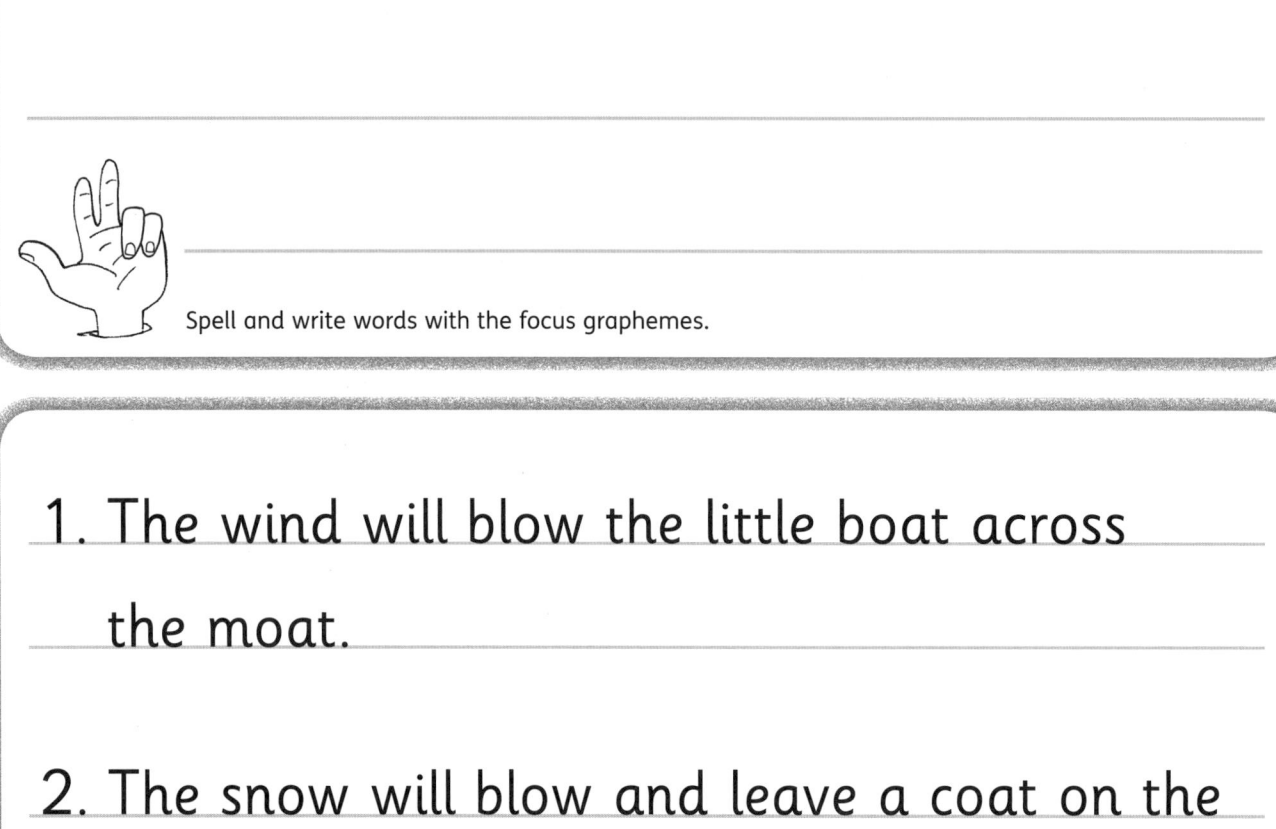

Spell and write words with the focus graphemes.

1. The wind will blow the little boat across the moat.

2. The snow will blow and leave a coat on the oak tree.

Blend to read the words and sentences.

Copy one of the sentences while saying the sounds of the words. Draw a picture to match the sentence.

Practise the sound

Say the sound. Trace the letters.

Say the sound. Trace the letters.

due   dew   rescue   few   newt

Tuesday   stew   re̲new   pewter

skewer   newborn   mildew   news

Sound out and blend to read the words.

_ _ _ _ _ _ _ _

_ _ _ _ _ _ _ _

_ _ _ _ _ _ _ _

Say the words. Spell the words. Write the words.

Practise your reading and writing

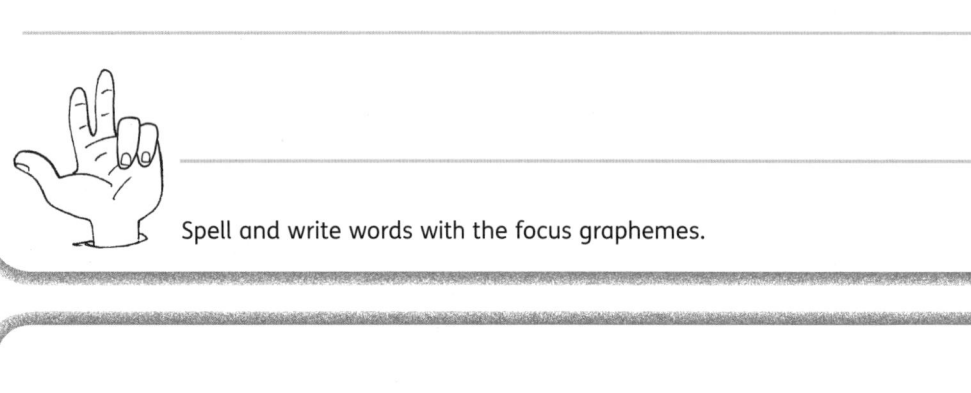

Spell and write words with the focus graphemes.

1. There are a few new pegs in the box.

2. The newt slips on its way to the pond.

    We rescue it.

Blend to read the words and sentences.

Copy one of the sentences while saying the sounds of the words. Draw a picture to match the sentence.

Practise the sound

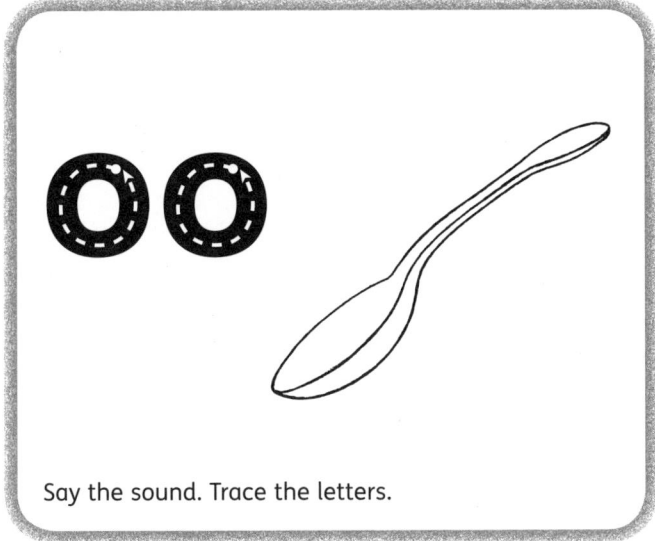

Say the sound. Trace the letters.

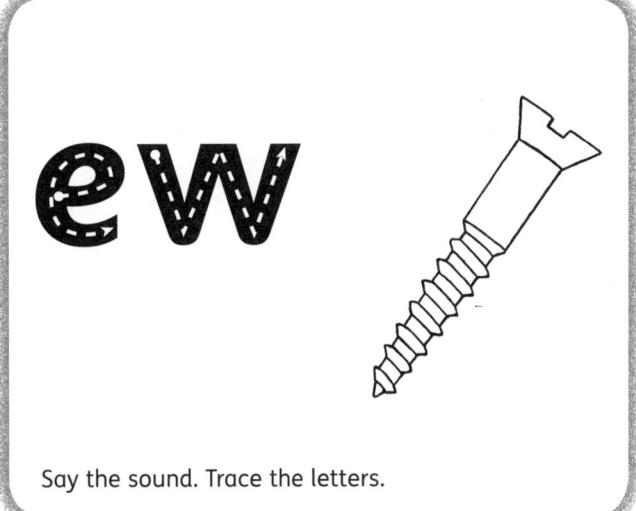

Say the sound. Trace the letters.

mood   yew   hoop   chew   threw

balloon   drew   crew   flew

brew   grew   shrew   screws

chewing   cashew nuts   shrewd

Sound out and blend to read the words.

___ ___

_____ ___   _____ ___ ___ ___

Say the words. Spell the words. Write the words.

Practise your reading and writing

Spell and write words with the focus graphemes.

1. Wilma flew to the moon in a big

blue balloon.

2. Chip went on a ship and was soon one

of the crew.

Blend to read the words and sentences.

Copy one of the sentences while saying the sounds of the words. Draw a picture to
match the sentence.

Practise the sound

Say the sound. Trace the letters.

Say the sound. Trace the letters.

bow   out   how   ouch   cow   loud

pouch   mouse   shout   south

sound   found   house   about

Sound out and blend to read the words.

Say the words. Spell the words. Write the words.

Practise your reading and writing

Spell and write words with the focus graphemes.

1. "That owl has a loud hoot," said my brother.

2. What shall we do? Shall we go out to town and hang around?

Blend to read the words and sentences.

Copy one of the sentences while saying the sounds of the words. Draw a picture to match the sentence.

Practise the sound

Say the sound. Trace the letters.

Say the sound. Trace the letters.

fur fir tree turn girls curls dirt

shirt stir firm thirteen skirt

birthday twirl thirsty third

Sound out and blend to read the words.

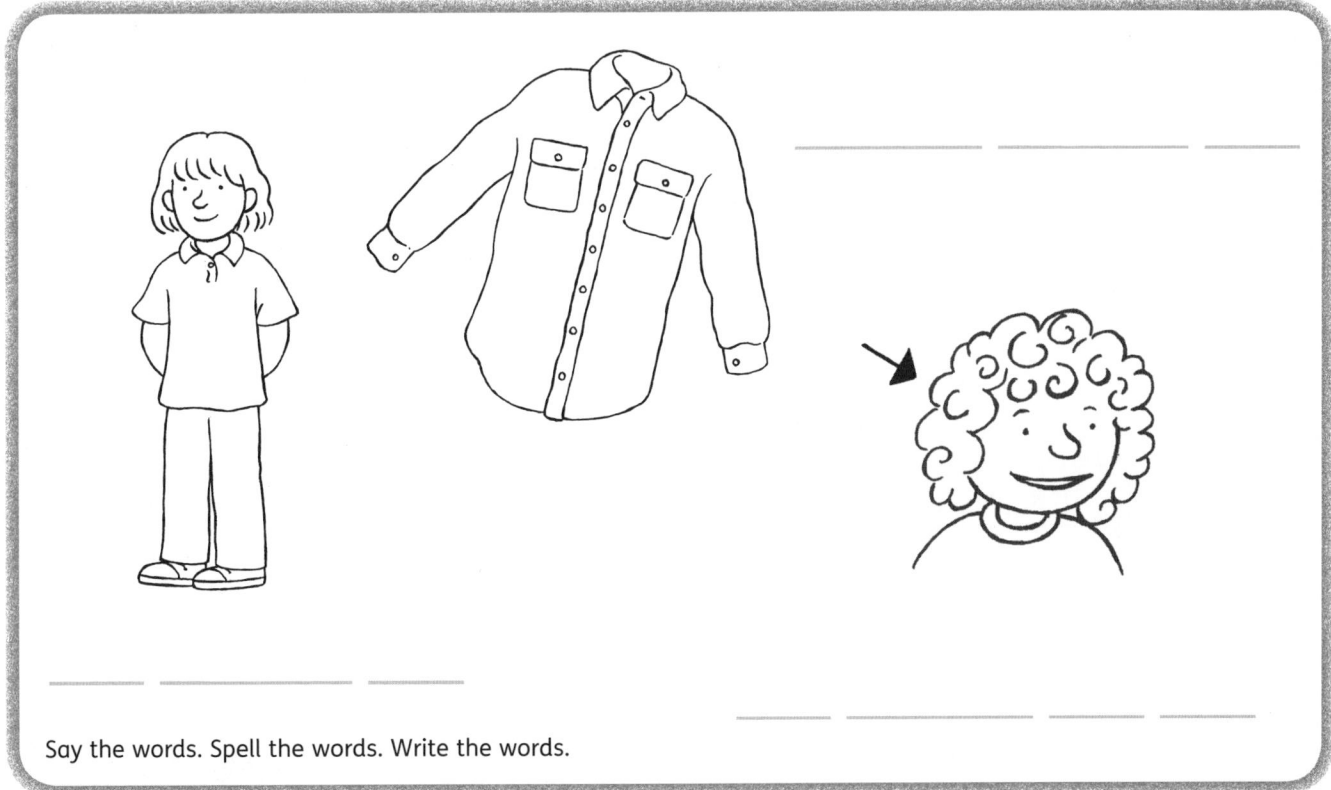

Say the words. Spell the words. Write the words.

Practise your reading and writing

/ur/ **ur** **ir**

Spell and write words with the focus graphemes.

1. First Biff got out her black skirt and then she got out her purple shirt.

2. When is it my turn to stir the flapjack mix?

Blend to read the words and sentences.

Copy one of the sentences while saying the sounds of the words. Draw a picture to match the sentence.

Practise the sound

Say the sound. Trace the letters.

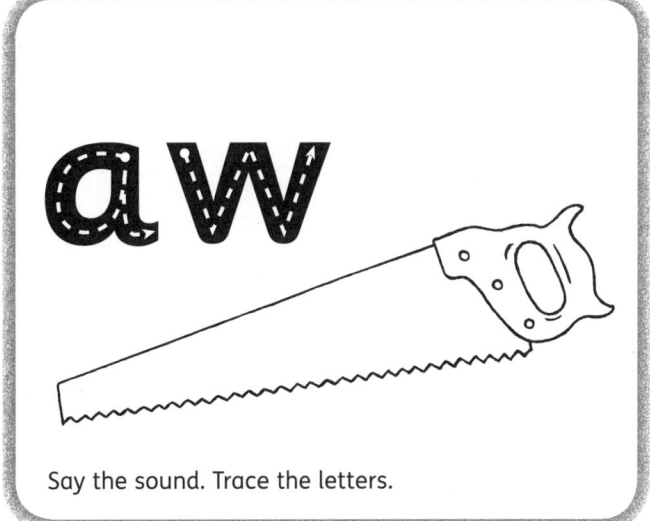

Say the sound. Trace the letters.

cork   paw   form   raw   port   jaws

lawn   thaws   draw   claw   hawk

prawns   straw   squawk   fawn

Sound out and blend to read the words.

Say the words. Spell the words. Write the words.

Practise your reading and writing

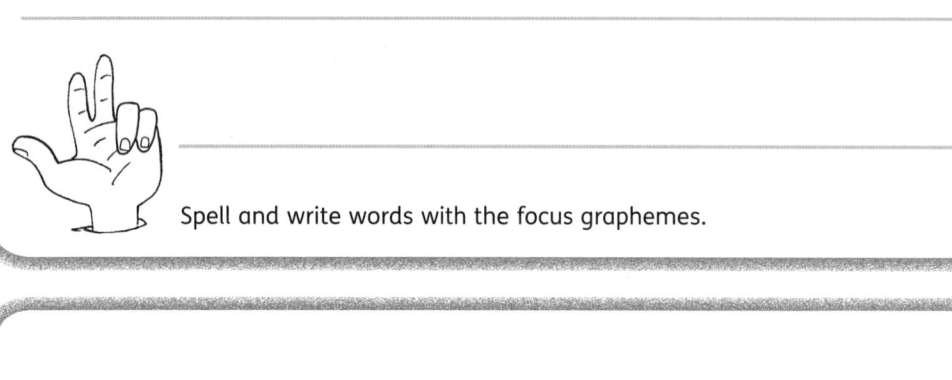

Spell and write words with the focus graphemes.

1. My cat has hurt his paw and must go to the vet.

2. I saw some black clouds so I think there will be a storm.

Blend to read the words and sentences.

Copy one of the sentences while saying the sounds of the words. Draw a picture to match the sentence.

Practise the sound

Say the sound. Trace the letters.

Say the sound. Trace the letters.

dear   deer   appear   jeer   shears

sheer   clear   sneer   steers

cheerful   puppeteer   mountaineer

Sound out and blend to read the words.

Say the words. Spell the words. Write the words.

Practise your reading and writing

Spell and write words with the focus graphemes.

1. The deer fears the hunter and runs away from the clearing.

2. The crowd cheer when they see a herd of deer appear.

Blend to read the words and sentences.

Copy one of the sentences while saying the sounds of the words. Draw a picture to match the sentence.

Practise the sound

Say the sound. Trace the letters.

Say the sound. Trace the letters.

fair   bus fare   hair   hare   chair

care   mare   shares   scared

stare   glares   flared   squares

Sound out and blend to read the words.

Say the words. Spell the words. Write the words.

Practise your reading and writing

Spell and write words with the focus graphemes.

1. Scare the birds away with a scarecrow!

2. My hair looks a mess and might scare you!

Blend to read the words and sentences.

Copy one of the sentences while saying the sounds of the words. Draw a picture to match the sentence.

Practise the sound

s

Say the sound. Trace the letters.

ce

Say the sound. Trace the letters.

swim   pence   skip   price   sing

fence   choice   force   bounce

office   fleece   voice   peaceful

Sound out and blend to read the words.

Say the words. Spell the words. Write the words.

Practise your reading and writing

Spell and write words with the focus grapheme.

1. Can I have ten pence for the sweet shop?

2. The prince says we must stand next to the fence and sing!

Blend to read the words and sentences.

Copy one of the sentences while saying the sounds of the words. Draw a picture to match the sentence.

Practise the sound

Say the sound. Trace the letters.

Say the sound. Trace the letters.

bed head melt read desk

bread dread ready thread

instead weather dreadful

Sound out and blend to read the words.

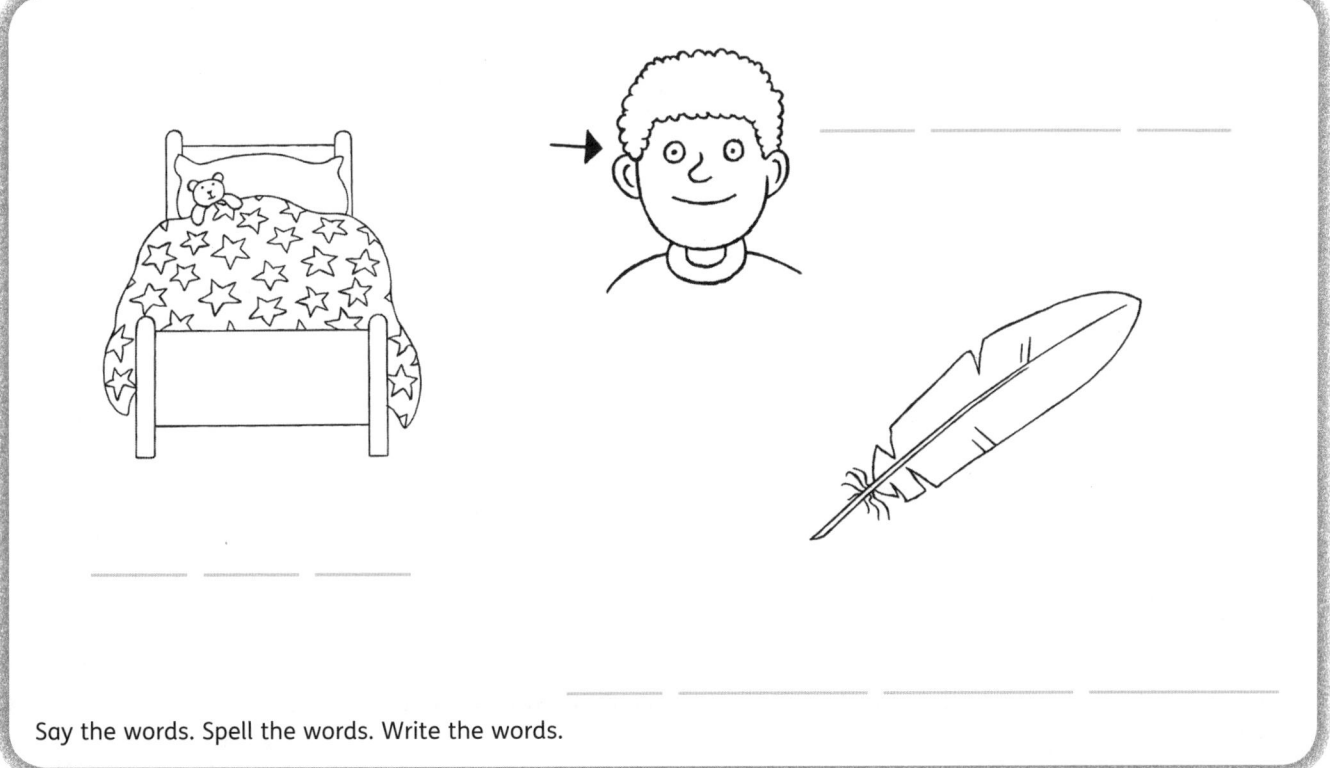

Say the words. Spell the words. Write the words.

Practise your reading and writing

Spell and write words with the focus grapheme.

1. The hen pecks at the bits of bread.

2. My tent is so little that I will bang my head
   if I stand up in it!

Blend to read the words and sentences.

Copy one of the sentences while saying the sounds of the words. Draw a picture to
match the sentence.

Practise the sound

u

Say the sound. Trace the letters.

o

Say the sound. Trace the letters.

sun   son   sum   other   luck   won

onion   welcoming   front   Monday

wonderful   mother   London

Sound out and blend to read the words.

Say the words. Spell the words. Write the words.

Practise your reading and writing

Spell and write words with the focus grapheme.

1. Jump for joy as we have won the cup!

2. The mother duck jumps in the mud and
   now she is a mucky duck!

Blend to read the words and sentences.

Copy one of the sentences while saying the sounds of the words. Draw a picture to
match the sentence.

Practise the sound

<table>
<tr>
<td>

ed

/d/ played

Say the sound. Say the word.

</td>
<td>

ed

/t/ dropped

Say the sound. Say the word.

</td>
</tr>
</table>

rained   stayed   grabbed

frowned   slipped   jumped

stopped   scratched   shrugged

owned   limped   stamped

Sound out and blend to read the words.

Say the words. Spell the words. Write the words.

Practise your reading and writing

-ed /d/ /t/

Spell and write words with the focus grapheme.

1. Mum helped me as I stepped up on the tree trunk.

2. We huffed, puffed and strained as we heaved the heavy box.

Blend to read the words and sentences.

Copy one of the sentences while saying the sounds of the words. Draw a picture to match the sentence.

ea   ew   oi -are o

-ue   ur   air   u   ee

ow   ou   eer   -ea

oa   ow   s   e -ay

-ie -ew   aw -ce ai

-ed -igh -oo or

oy   ir   -ed ear

Oxford Reading Tree

Floppy's Phonics

Oxford Level 4

Activity Book 4

Say the sounds and practise your reading, spelling and handwriting skills.

Text © Oxford University Press
© Phonics International Ltd 2020

Illustrations by Oxford Designers and Illustrators

Cover Illustration by Alex Brychta

The characters in this work are the original creation of Roderick Hunt and Alex Brychta who retain copyright in the characters.

First published 2011
This edition published 2020

ISBN 978-1-38-200559-3

10 9 8
Printed in China

Paper used in the production of this book is a natural, recyclable product made from wood grown in sustainable forests. The manufacturing process conforms to the environmental regulations of the country of origin.

The manufacturer's authorised representative in the EU for product safety is Oxford University Press España S.A. of El Parque Empresarial San Fernando de Henares, Avenida de Castilla, 2 – 28830 Madrid (www.oup.es/en or product. safety@oup.com). OUP España S.A. also acts as importer into Spain of products made by the manufacturer.

Oxford OWL Helping your child's learning with free eBooks, essential tips and fun activities
www.oxfordowl.co.uk

OXFORD
UNIVERSITY PRESS
₹195

How to get in touch:
web www.oxfordprimary.co.uk
email primary.enquiries@oup.com
tel. +44 (0) 1536 452610
fax +44 (0) 1865 313472

ISBN 978-1-38-200559-3

9 781382 005593